Unleashing Your

Inner Dog

Unleashing Your Inner Dog

Your Best Friend's Guide to Life

Mari Gayatri Stein

New World Library
Novato, California

 New World Library
14 Pamaron Way
Novato, California 94949

Grateful acknowledgment is made to Coleman Barks for use of the verse appearing on page 35 from *Like This* © copyright 1990 by Coleman Barks (Athens, Ga.: Maypop, 1990).

The art appeaing on pages xii, 24, 112 appeared in slightly different form in *The Buddha Smiles* © copyright 1999 by Mari Gayatri Stein. Used by permission of White Cloud Press.

Library of Congress Cataloging-in-Publication Data
Stein, Mari, 1947–
    Unleashing your inner dog : your best friend's guide to life / art and text by Mari Gayatri Stein.
        p. cm.
    ISBN 1-57731-165-5 (alk. paper)
1. Dogs. 2. Dogs — Pictorial works. 3. Dogs in art. I. Title.
SF426.2 .S69 2001
636.7'0022'2 — dc21   00-011142

First Printing, March, 2001
ISBN 1-57731-165-5
Printed in Singapore on acid-free paper
Distributed to the trade by Publishers Group West

10 9 8 7 6 5 4 3 2 1

To all beings,

may we realize our true dog nature, which is love.

Love transcends form.

CONTENTS

I can take my dog anywhere.

⁂ INTRODUCTION

Seeking and seeing are worlds apart. This is the story of how our dogs can rescue us from a life of delusion and instruct us in the art of love and joy. By observing our canine companions, we can learn to be our own top dog.

For my whole life, I have been looking for a way to dwell with the angels while continuing to delight in earthly pleasures (the lovely squishiness of digging my toes into wet earth, gobbling a juicy peach, falling in love under the full moon, inhaling a gardenia, cuddling and rolling with my dogs on the floor). This wanting to press the veil and merge with the muse led me astray again and again. I tried to find my way back home but kept encountering yet another mirage of hope. I continued to yearn for the love beyond longing, intimacy beyond talking, transcendence beyond aging, and a taste of the lips of the gods. But all my wholesome intentions fell short, for in my desire to be happy I failed to recognize what was true to my heart and genuine in my soul.

One day as I sat dejected and in a quandary over why the ethers had failed to materialize after all my efforts, my dog Moon tiptoed thoughtfully to my side. She wore a look of compassion so spacious the ocean could not compete. Her gentle expression, both wise and patient, told me it was time to set down my vigilant quest and pet my dog. Under the influence of Moon's silent instruction, solace disrobed herself. Clarity dawned. At last my long-awaited vision had appeared.

Moon brought my world into new focus; my senses awoke to the gift of

Home is where your dog is.

being alive. Here was my muse, my guru, the love eager to light my way. The jewel had been concealed in the most obvious of places. All the answers lay here in the lap of my dogs, right in the den of my house. As it turned out, the sacred abode where my heart dwelled had four paws, a muzzle, and a tail.

Then the doctor said I was likely to die unless I had open-heart surgery. Time was panting and so were my five dogs. My motley crew rallied. They gathered around me and assured me it was not too late. They were going to lead me home to safety and show me how to unleash my inner dog. Their belief was empowering, and I was ready to surrender my ego and become a disciple.

I discovered our dogs have the wherewithal to reroute our lives. They can provide us with a new map to happiness. Our dogs are in fact our best friends, our guides to life. These seers of the soul have the power to inspire us to our highest good. They incite us to beneficent action and flood us with the spirit of generosity, gratitude, and faith. Our canine cohorts bring out the best in us; they also have a talent for making the most out of the worst in us. Dog consciousness dashes all duality and untangles truth from delusion. Our holy hounds teach us how to sing life's gospel in full voice. Through the observation of our dogs, we learn to discard the symbols and become the song. They show us how to slip the collar and unmuzzle our creativity, to experience the thrill of naked authenticity.

Our dogs are our gurus.

The week before my surgery, our eldest dog Moss died. The household was in mourning. Bereft, we all moped around, too sad to worry about my upcoming ordeal. On the raw December morning we headed off to the hospital, I carried with me the angel drawing of Moss and Megan (that appears on page 81). Someone posted it nearby my bed. When they wheeled me into the surgery, I knew my canine guardian angels would be watching over me as I hovered between worlds. I imagined us frolicking together in the ethers and tickling the stars.

Now, my mechanically ticking heart beats testimony to the wondrous technology of the millennium, and the scar that divides my chest bears witness to the dogged courage and faith inspired by my eternal companions. With each click of my heart, I visualize Megan and Moss keeping time with their tails. Isn't it true that all of our dogs remain a part of our hearts forever?

When you are in dog, you dare to let your petticoats fly.

LA LA LA LA LA

We are everything to our dogs. They recognize us. We do not need to earn their love. We already fill the infinite horizons of their view.

Our dogs teach us how to think with our hearts and love with our minds. They show us how to embrace what has been unloved for so long. They fetch back that lost thread of awareness that allows us to be at one with the world. They relentlessly protect us from our wayward selves and help us to decipher their bone mots. When we listen, our dogs speak to us with the silent voice of truth. They never sit in judgment, snigger, or go behind our backs and tell tales. They wag us on no matter how many times we falter.

In the company of dogs, we are able to be at ease and express our innate happiness. We stop hoarding ourselves. We begin to rejoice in each other's good fortune and act compassionately toward all beings of all breeds.

WAG WAG WAG..

Wag us on!

Our furry friends give us permission to lie down and rest without having to get sick first. They teach us how to be real and regale in our puppylike nature.

They invite us to be exuberant and playful without needing a reason. Our dogs can teach us how to relax. Their bark is like a mindfulness bell ringing us back to merciful understanding and the effulgence of Now. They show us how to be forgiving, free and fearless without being victimized, foolish, and reckless. Under our dogs' protection we dare to relax our guard and trust again, to lap up every delicious drop of the precious time allotted us.

Humans have a lot to learn about being blissful and vibrant. Studying our dogs is an assignment of the highest order, a meditation technique nonpareil.

You can always trust your dog not to hurt your heart.

We realize that our true dog nature is love. We too are a beloved and essential part of the pack — and highly prized.

If we could see with a dog's eye view, listen with their intuitive wisdom, and speak with their humor and instinct, the world would be a Shangrr-la indeed. We probably forfeited any chance of being as evolved as our dogs when our tails dropped off. Such a pity.

Come! Let us romp, wag, and roll through these pages together, sniff out the truth, revive our hearts, and tickle our fantasies. Let us dine well on every image, arf, and grrr. And if we're still hungry at the end, we can always lie down together and gnaw on the cover for awhile. As devout dog devotees, we will be able to live in harmony with one another. We will excel in the art of being ourselves and burst forth with the aliveness of the moment, our hearts so full they hardly hold their love. Now as initiated members of the pack, we will rediscover how to wag the memory of a tail long gone.

Regaling in our puppylike nature.

Sometimes you act as though a fish

is swimming away with your brain.

WHAT IS THE COLOR OF WOOF?

HOW MANY TAILS DO YOU SEE?

HAPPY ON THE
GROUND.
A SIMPLE
MOMENT OF
HAPPINESS.

CHAPTER 1

JOIE DE VIVRE

Dogs have mastered the art of joy. They are malleable, allowing themselves to be transformed by life and ripened gracefully, while we humans are forever trying to change, orchestrate, and control our world.

Why worry when you can have fun in the sky?

Our dogs have the ability to transmute conflict and difficulty into gold.

When the fur is flying,

use it as a moustache.

When we are feeling depressed and aggrieved, they entreat us to offer ourselves empathy, compassion, and forgiveness. When we are caught up in embarrassment, they immediately banish our wince waves and teach us how to enjoy laughing at ourselves, right out loud.

The joys of running free in your imagination.

Human beings everywhere know terrible suffering and despair. When people disagree and resist, they go to war — war with themselves and war with one another.

Choose a mediator who is impartial

NOW JUST TRY TO LISTEN WITHOUT GETTING ALL WAGGED UP.

and knows you both inside and out.

Dogs may defend their territory, but it arises out of a sense of duty and their earnest desire to be of service, never malevolence.

Dogs have elevated the art of combat by taking the war out of the war

Defending your person.

game. Resistance to a dog is a game of tug-of-war with a squeaky bunny or your favorite sock (new and white, most likely). Terrorizing a stick is the most malicious act in which they will ever engage. Who cares who wins? It doesn't matter. Just the thrill of playing well is the point. When they finish the game and someone runs with the prize, they pick it up, shake it all about, and start fresh.

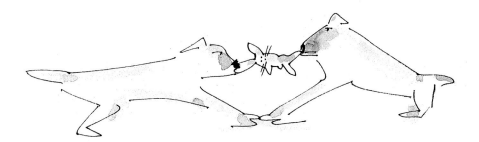

When I watch Morgan roll in the grass and see every aspect of life anew with innocent eyes, even though he can hardly distinguish shapes through his cataracts, it reminds me that, indeed, life is precious, life is short. I realize I must be overdue for a good delve in the rose garden too.

Time is fleeting. Hang onto your dog.

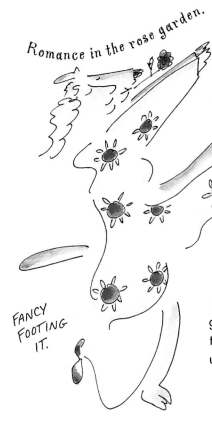

Romance in the rose garden.

FANCY
FOOTING
IT.

When I used to watch Moss gleefully return the ball again and again, infusing each boomerang activity with new delight, it was a reminder to cultivate the art of contentment while performing the simple, repetitive tasks to which I have sadly become jaded and grown a scaly armor of aversion.

Dogs are the masters of complete experience. They are eclectic in their aliveness. With relish and gusto, they embrace whatever adventure life offers up, and then relinquish it completely without lingering desire, brooding, or remorse. They are tenacious in the pursuit of their passions and unafraid to take risks.

Basking in the afterglow.

Unlike most of us, they can bask in the afterglow of experience, enjoying its enrichment as part of the fiber of their being, woven through them in the wholesome and wise ways of Mother Nature.

Dogs teach us how to live with true joie de vivre and to receive our bounty of well-being as naturally as we would greet an old friend who had been kept waiting patiently in the corridor for a very long time. Anyone who has ever blotted her lipstick on her dog's nose knows bliss, or cuddled on the carpet immersed in their divine furriness knows fulfillment. Surely it surpasses candlelight, éclairs, and homemade coconut ice cream.

CHAPTER 2

UNCONDITIONAL LOVE AND DEVOTION

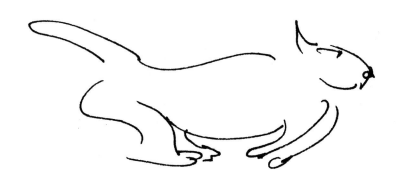

Dogs would if they could—actually they do it all the time.

My dogs can look into my eyes with the purity and courage only a realized being could emulate. Love gives life meaning and dogs are pure love. Love in canine spaces.

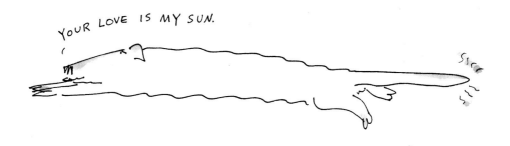

YOUR LOVE IS MY SUN.

Uncomplicated and pure of heart and motive, our companions fearlessly accompany us through births and deaths, sickness and health. They are consistently kindhearted, generous, and devoted. They teach us to trust. We can depend on their love.

They are unflappable no matter how wildly we emote. Their uncompromised devotion instructs us in the art of loving, free of judgment and without a price tag. Our dogs are sensitive to our every whim.

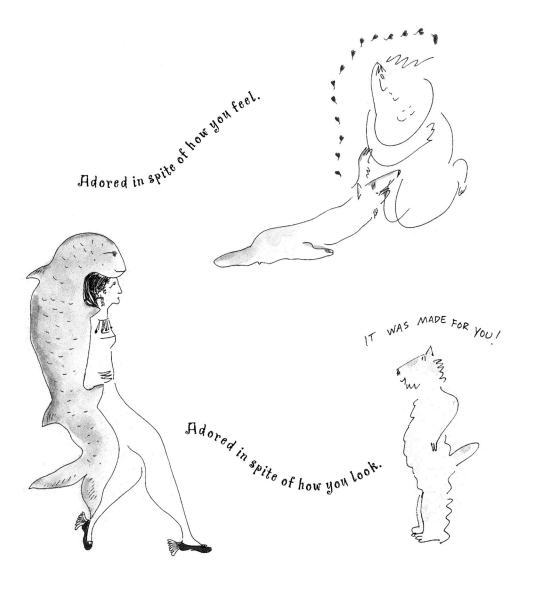

Adored in spite of how you feel.

Adored in spite of how you look.

IT WAS MADE FOR YOU!

How is it they know just when to nuzzle up close and when to sit and watch from afar with fixed eyes of affection? Their love gives us X-ray vision. We begin to see through worldly disguises and defenses. Dog-love takes us home to the heart and provides an ever ready prescription for happiness. When we are in turmoil and in danger of making a mess of our lives, our canine comrades instinctively show us how to let the mud settle, revel in it, roll around, and then shake it all off. With a gentle but firm probe of the nose, they hold us in place and surround us with the presence of loving kindness that protects us from our foolish selves.

Reminiscing over dog-love makes us feel as though our whole body is smiling.

When you can't comfort yourself, your dog can be a great help. Anytime I am lonely and blue, full of longing, and given to tears, my dogs stage a feel-good review. Enter Moon who immediately flattens her furry mass into an alligator-basking-in-the-sun-spread-out pose. She rests there, her head between her paws, pink tongue protruding like a rose petal.

"Come on, let's play." Wag, wag, wag. "I'm waiting," her eager eyes implore as they bore into mine without a blink.

Mulph, taking her cue in the wings, ceremoniously grabs her tail between her legs, which slightly elevates her derrière and begins her dervish whirl, bouncing herself up and down as though she would launch into orbit. It is the most preposterously zany dog-dance I have ever seen, and I find myself smiling through my self-absorption and laughing with reckless abandon.

Soothing your mistress.

When you are in love, time stands still.

DON'T WORRY ABOUT SAVING THESE SONGS!
AND IF ONE OF OUR INSTRUMENTS BREAKS,
IT DOESN'T MATTER.
WE HAVE FALLEN INTO THE PLACE
WHERE EVERYTHING IS MUSIC. - RUMI

When someone loves you, you dare to fall in love with yourself again.

Dogs have mastered the art of loving well. There is nothing petty about our pups. Revenge is not in their vocabulary. Enthrall is. If we were more like our dogs, the world would be a better place. They are able to bring effort without tension, to give without expectation, to be present in the joy of the moment, to be fulfilled. There is nothing muddy about the love bond we feel with our dogs, except the dog itself.

Dog love is clear and unconditional, simple and heartfelt, creatively innocent and yet as natural, easy, and familiar to us as our own toes. Dogs elicit our compassionate response. They show us how to give selflessly and to receive graciously. Maybe if we are able to remain attentive and teachable, we will be reborn into their magical circle of loving devotion and aliveness, and grow into the kinds of beings they have always believed us to be.

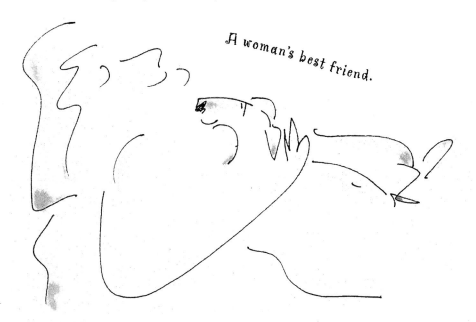

A woman's best friend.

HICCUP.

REVELING IN LIFE'S ABUNDANCE

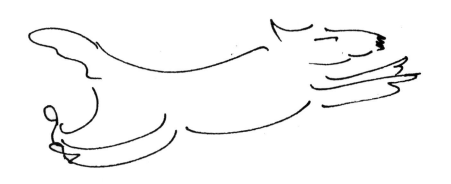

EVERYDAY IS A CELEBRATION!

Allow yourself to become a silken thread in the garment of earth and ether.

Life with dogs is inclusive, never exclusive. Why not have it all, they declare with a jaunty wag! Dance around yourself. Be gleeful. Put your restraint away and let's play. Who has more right to celebrate? (Except your dog, of course.) Come on. Let's roll in the grass. Dig a hole. Sniff out a mole. Chew up a shoe. And don't be ashamed to whimper when you get a burr in your paw.

Who else but your furry friend can instantly alert you to the wonder of it all with a simple woof? When you're in the pooh, who can you trust to give you a paw up without fail? Dogs revel in the glory of life's abundance. They know how to live on the edge of silly. That which is divine becomes tangible in their midst.

They exude gratitude with every windshield-wiper wag of their tails, and clear away the mists of our discontent.

Offering your palms as a cup to receive celestial tea.

Your dog is more direct.

Sometimes a little indulgence is a boon to the psyche.
Re: The art of not taking yourself too seriously.

Learning the secrets of insects while your dog drinks martinis.

Why do we humans feel inherently guilty about enjoying ourselves? What a squander; we are so misspent. In dogdom, every sense is an invitation to a rare kind of rapture. A new discovery. Nothing is wasted. Each morning offers fresh delights. Dawn arrives and my dogs rally at the den door, tap-dancing feverishly, hardly contained by their forms. I am greeted with the fierce pleasure of first love, the debut of another grand reunion. (You'd think I'd just returned from an around-the-world cruise.) Once acknowledged, I can't open the door fast enough as they gyrate in anticipation of the crunch of the first biscuit, the thrill of the pungent morning grass, the invigorating roll in that delicious muck that reawakens all that is primal.

Distinctly they tell me to pay attention, stop drooping, whining, and wishing for what I think is missing. They remind me to relish the warmth of my bed, that first sip of tea, the sound of my heartbeat, and the view through the window of my furry foursome stretching with ecstasy and then racing to explore the wonder of some new extravagant smell and sound. I find I am even able to savor the flavor of the cleansing tear from missing my mom, as it rolls down my cheek.

Dogs do not live in a world of half measures. Happy or sad, they show us how to escape into life and live it intensely. Intoxicated by the infinite possibilities of all experience, their wholeness makes them fearlessly willing to take a big bite out of whatever fruit life bears.

EAU DE DUNG.

Loss and disappointment become a cathartic revelation of pure feeling, a cleansing that invites us to breathe in the miracle of both birth and death.

Our dogs show us how to die into pain without shame and without taking it personally. They expose sorrow's virtue as the consort of joy. They offer us a

Springtime fancies.

cloak of courage; our armor becomes as soft as their fur coats. They teach us to reclaim all parts of ourselves, to make merry with life's munificent bequests, to glory in love without fear of our hearts shattering. When we find ourselves refugees from the domain of a broken heart, our dogs show us there are still amazing and unexplored territories in which to revel. In our coexistence, we see it is possible to have a good life and a good death, too. Their benevolence and wisdom continue to speak to us from beyond the grave.

To grieve the death of a dog is to feel the ground fall away from under our feet, but it is also a loss cleanly felt — truly a wrench, but free of the judgments, guilt, and regret that surround the death of a relative or friend. Although it is a rent never completely repaired, we become more spacious beings because of it, rejoined with the great cycle of life that spins us in its orbit. Our dogs remain a part of our hearts, instilled in our souls. In the wake of their shining spirit, we understand that feeling pain through, as nature intended, is liberating and cleansing. We feel as though a fallow part of our being is suddenly enriched and able to grow a tender plant of magical blooms.

Drunk with roses, agog with Mother Nature's gifts.

PANACHE

46

Taking a tentative step toward death.

MAYBE DEATH IS A BIG CUDDLY DOG.

Our dogs can identify their happiness. There is no pretense about going after what they want and flaunting their success. This helps me to stop apologizing for the good that befalls me and allows me to appreciate with humility what life offers up.

Dogs are effervescent, fuzzy marvels of nature. As we begin to emulate their richness in living, we find like them, we have become infectious in our happiness, drawing all around us into our realm of joy. We begin loving and loving and loving all those parts of ourselves so we never have to feel homeless again.

"Nothing is real, so stop taking yourself so seriously. Woofie."

She's a real prize!

Dogs know what they want.

CHAPTER 4

AUTHENTICITY

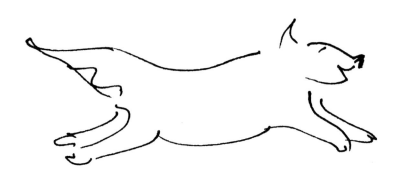

With our dogs, what we get is more than what we ordinarily are able to see.
The pooch package is complete. The batteries are included, the jam too. There are no extras to order, hidden agendas, or missing amenities. À la carte does not exist in the canine kingdom. Dogs are genuine, authentic in their essential dogness.

NO EMPTY CALORIES

I'M THE GENUINE THING

I'M CERTIFIED ORGANIC

DON'T IT MAKE YOU WANNA SING

Dogs are pure nourishment.

Their every breath is one of vital aliveness. Dogself-consciousness is so pure that their Self never gets in the way. Their thoughts, woofs, and actions fall from them as unpretentiously as ripe figs from the tree. They enjoy clarity, insight, and

Honest to a faux paw.

humor in all their endeavors. Their senses are superlative. Their noses naturally sniff out the truth. In our earnest pursuit of the truth, we tend to step over it. Our dogs force us to step into it. While we are awkwardly tripping over ourselves, our dogs show us how to get out of our own way and get on with the job of living life unremittingly. Dogs effortlessly exhibit an ease of well-being that philosophers and seekers have thirsted after for eternity. Our steadfast pals are unafraid to show their true feelings.

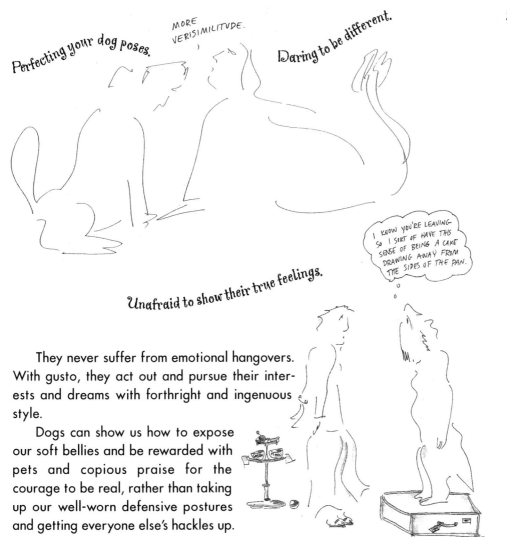

Perfecting your dog poses.

MORE VERISIMILITUDE.

Daring to be different.

Unafraid to show their true feelings.

I KNOW YOU'RE LEAVING SO I SORT OF HAVE THIS SENSE OF BEING A CAKE DRAWING AWAY FROM THE SIDES OF THE PAN.

They never suffer from emotional hangovers. With gusto, they act out and pursue their interests and dreams with forthright and ingenuous style.

Dogs can show us how to expose our soft bellies and be rewarded with pets and copious praise for the courage to be real, rather than taking up our well-worn defensive postures and getting everyone else's hackles up.

54   How easy it is to make lifetime vows to these inspirational marvels of nature. With innocent delight and a passion free of selfish desire, we honor, care for, and obey our dogs with an eagerness and gratification we rarely display while attending to our own needs.

When wagging becomes an issue.

In their gentle way, they teach us how to be ourselves. "You'll never do anyone else nearly as well," they remind us with a full-tilt grin.

We can easily accept the foibles of dogdom. They unleash a life force untainted by judgment and fear. Dogs are at peace with their primal nature. They inherently know how to sort out the difficult issues of survival in a straightforward and lyrical way. They teach us that living our truth saves time. With efficiency and a practical approach, they establish a pecking order, choose a leader of the pack, engage in sex, and enjoy food and relaxation with a lust for life and inevitability that achieves its own balance by being authentic. Somehow we human beings manage to sour our humaneness by constantly trying to rise above our humanness, to live outside of ourselves, to conquer nature. In the face of all the evidence of the eons, we continue to take ourselves seriously and sacrifice the joys and truth of the moment in an effort to pretend we will never die. If we could be as real as our dogs, not only would we be sporting a tail, a long muzzle, and ears, but we'd be wagging all the time.

WHAT BREED ARE YOU?

BONE FIDO!

BASICALLY I LIKE DOING THINGS WITH YOU
AS LONG AS YOU DO WHAT I WANT
TO DO, WHICH AT THIS PRECISE
MOMENT IN TIME HAPPENS TO BE NOTHING.

CHAPTER 5

ACCEPTANCE AND CONTENTMENT

DOG GRANT ME THE SERENITY
TO ACCEPT THE THINGS I CANNOT CHANGE
THE COURAGE TO CHANGE THE THINGS I CAN
AND THE WISDOM TO KNOW
THE DIFFERENCE.

Dogs always show their true colors.

From the time of puppyhood, dogs are blessed with a talent for following their instincts. When they are up and doing, it is in agreement with Mother Nature. Our hounds have the inborn ability to recycle the energy wasted in pushing against life.

Be an instrument of Mother Nature lest you remain unused.

They don't stand and argue with the way things are.

They know how to find comfort by living life on life's terms. With a wag of gratitude and a wisdom beyond their dog years, they are able to rephrase life's sentences and translate them into their own tongue, which flows with the melodious voice of acceptance, contentment, and joyous consent. Every canine action is an attraction. By following in their paw prints, we find ourselves reformed and dwelling in a state of easy acceptance.

No matter how annoying a new puppy may be, whining through the night, peeing everywhere in sight — and out of sight — and chewing everything in reach, we find her irresistible and adorable. Dogs are irritation erasers. Their need for us dissolves all bastions of resistance. The gift of a dog is a grace bestowed.

A dog's nose is a thing of grace.

— I'M A TEAM PLAYER.

No matter how demanding their care, we are contented to be at their service.

We might find ourselves apologizing to our dogs or making excuses, but we never really have to. In time, they teach us to extend this trait of magnanimous self-acceptance to include the entire world.

Dogs know that in an impermanent world, every flavor, hue, and view of life is shared — a communal experience. A sense of oneness is inbred. Nothing belongs to them (except our hearts, of course). In their self-accord, they draw us closer. They teach us how to relax in the face of adversity, shake off our mistakes

Esprit de corps!

with humility and humor, and let life's current carry us along in silken tranquility.

We have a lot to learn from our effervescent, fuzzy friends. When bad things happen to good dogs, they take time to pant wildly, give off a good grrr, perhaps chow down on your newest shoe, indulge in a scowl and short-termed sulk compressed in a corner (tail view in your direction) and then in a blink, lap loudly from the commode, and get on with the job of survival.

DRAWING INTO YOURSELF
FOR A LONG SLEEP
AFTER A LONG TIME OF GRIEF.
(YOUR DOG SWINGS ALONG
LIKE A STAR ON THE MOON.)

Dogs don't have preferences and all dogs are stars.

IN A TIZZ ONE MOMENT...

IN A SYLVAN TRANCE
THE NEXT

Unlike us, they never suffer from bad-dog syndrome. They are
not resentment collectors. They can discriminate between wholesome remorse
and guilt. To them guilt is a useless emotion, selfish, indulgent, and a time waster.
Dog awareness is unhindered by self-righteous delusion. Their mission is to meld
the separation of right and wrong and good and bad, and
transform it into wise and skillful action. In an
instant, they can make amends with
the loving offer of a lick or a vase-
shattering wag and perhaps that
old seasoned bone they've been
saving up for a special celebra-
tion. That done, everyone

shakes paws contentedly and is ready to begin again. With acceptance, they are able to create a moment of justice in an unjust world and exhale a breath of cool contentment.

In an effort to be right and get our own way, we become disenfranchised. We feel cut off from our opportunity to be secure, serene, even rapturous. Our dogs show us how foolish it is to fight the flow.

By their example we begin to reclaim the calories eaten up by our refusals to accept the way things are. Instead we begin to embrace the moment and enjoy our just due of gladness.

A minor disagreement can ruin the whole day, but dogs never go to bed mad.

In step with life's refrain.

Woman seeking contentment dons magical dog turban.

Moon will expend concentrated energy on corralling all her toys and other bounty. She's a border collie. This trait is intrinsic to her nature. Piled up on her bed, chin resting high on the perch, she hoards her loot and guards her spoils with the delirious look of self-satisfaction that is almost a dare. But when the time comes to dispense the goodies among the brood, even though I observe a subtle shadow of doubt passing behind her eyes, it is soon forgotten as the gang gets going and the game begins. Pandemonium reigns as my red slipper, the fuzzy dinosaur, squeaky ball, muddy stick, and old sock fly around the bedroom. Our dogs show us that contentment is happiness in action as well as in repose. This inner repose is the seat of their contentment and arises naturally out of their acceptance of who and what they are and those about them.

To your dog, you are always enough.

A CUP OF TEA
THE MOON
AND THEE!

Knowing yourself, accept who you are.

Resistance causes suffering. Acceptance yields freedom, equanimity, and serenity. Herein lies a new and animated perspective. We begin to heal. We discover satisfaction and innovation growing where misery, malcontent, and tension used to fester. Even pain can instruct us in the linguistics of lyrical living and give

Always couturier.

us a language that reaches beyond our usual stunted vocabulary. Just pause to watch your dog create wonder out of disappointment, challenge out of frustration, compassion out of hurt. Even in sadness they find refuge. With equanimity they allow themselves and us to express and indulge our curiosities and desires utterly.

With relief this has given me permission to no longer apologize to my non-dog buddies for being a dog person. My friends are used to stepping over the biscuit crumbs, dog rugs, tangle of fuzzy toys, murdered squeakies, and deflated piffles that decorate my car and office. (To me they bring comfort, a contented sense of safety and homeliness. They are reassuring.) I do, however, protect dog-challenged acquaintances from my mob's love-siege greeting ritual. It is a well known fact that dog-deprived people

Our dogs' patience and obedience are saintlike.

BURP!

A BIG FAT CAT
PERCHES ON YOUR HAT
WHILE YOU FAN YOURSELF
WITH A BAT.

— BATS ARE
VERY COOLING.

YOUR DOG WAITS
OBEDIENTLY
FOR INSTRUCTIONS

SIGH

have to be brought around slowly and require patience and finessing with gloved paws.

Canine respect and acceptance of all our differences and unique personalities give birth to a new freedom and creativity. Dogs avidly endorse who we are. They don't care to trade in their personalities for new ones or to alter ours. They know how to capitalize on their dogness and remain flexible by not identifying with an illusive image. Dogs are not encumbered by the need to be fashionable and yet they never clash with nature. Their ensemble is always de rigueur.

Our canine compatriots embrace us with spaciousness and greet our eccentricities with equanimity. Distraction becomes an art form, not poisoned by the drivenness-to-be-doing-what-cannot-be-done. Our dogs' patience and obedience are saintlike. "It will all come to pass. Don't worry about a thing," they say with raised eyebrows and a jiggle of their ears. "Acceptance and contentment will be victorious over any foe."

When we finally are willing to let go, we enjoy rest and peace of soul. At last, we can curl up on our cushions with our dogs in a cozy donut pose. Acceptance brings out our graciousness, opens our hearts, and gives way to our natural perfection. Without acceptance there can be no happiness, no liberation, no peace, no contentment. Our dogs know this. To turn away from this law of dog nature and basic truth would be tantamount to turning an angel away.

Portly dog who exudes confidence.

I'M A CHUNKAMUNK AND PROUD OF IT.

You can have a bad day.

You can even be grumpy.

You just can't be grumpy about being grumpy

and having a bad day,

or you can but it won't amount to happiness.

CHAPTER 6

PRIORITIES AND JUST BEING IN THE NOW

An ablution of direct experience.

LIVING LIFE WITH APLOMB.

LIVING LIFE WITH A PLUM.

There is no time but the present. Our dogs live one woof at a time. They know how to mesh with the moment and bathe in the elation of direct experience. People look without seeing. We feel as though we are always missing out, that the meaning of our lives has vanished in the blink of an eye. For dogs, each blink is a rebirth. They remind us that we don't need to worry about growing up, but growing wise, or about getting there, but being here. Their minds and feelings, hearts and souls prevail in the same place as their noses, ears, tails, and four paws — and, most importantly, at the same time. Precious moments are

Don't you suppose everything really important happens

when we're blinking.

Red flag phrases for dogs.

savored. To them, time out is time lost. Human beings are humans doing, always preoccupied with planning ahead or juggling the past. We are forever looking forward to accomplishing this or reminiscing about that, sometimes with longing, often with regret, but rarely with the sense of completeness and fulfillment that comes from just being in the Now.

    "So . . . when does the arfing play begin?" our dog asks us, head cocked with winsome allure and paws anchored on earth. "Remember me? Bow wow! Make contact. Not a week from woof but right now."

    "There may not be another barking intermission. Touch life, tenderly but with abandon. There is no holding on, so why hold back? Bow wow! Can you feel that exquisite grrr-ping sensation moving up your spine? You are like a plant woofing for the sun. Now cup your furless paws together, raise them up to the sky, and let the heavens rain down and fill them with celestial wonder. Allow

yourself to thaw and enjoy the miracle of being with me here in the Right Now."

Our dogs are too smart to be put on a promise. If there is happiness to be had, by dog, it does not belong to the future. That instant gratification with which our Western culture has become obsessed to the point of dementia is always readily available when we simply come back to the present moment of experience, let our bodies soften, pay attention, and perk up our ears.

Dogs only do one thing at a time and all existence joins in. They can travel the world in a single gesture. At dusk, when they venture out to explore the latest mystery-creature-scent, the whole realm of their senses ignites. Defecating is an electrifying dance on the grass, a ritual of delight. Lapping water from the pond equals the excitement of coming upon an oasis after a long, thirsty trek in the desert.

We wholesale our dreams and try to erase the shame of selling ourselves short by acquiring the latest technology and making yet another list that promises that allusive answer to all our longing and guarantees to organize us into a state of true happiness.

"Follow me and I'll take you to a sacred barking place in your own backyard and teach you how to see properly. Can you dig it?"

At night we lie awake in turmoil, our weary minds atangle in a web of angst, trying out another strategy to tame the demons of the night and escape

Fetched back home for yourself.

HOME JEEVES.

the Devil's grip. My dogs have trained me well. Now I know what to do. I turn on the light and gaze over at Morgan who is splayed on the green sofa, his aging gray muzzle snuggled into a cushion. He radiates the dizzy sweetness of untroubled sleep — the inno-cent, yearned-for sleep unawares. Once again, he has offered the gift of just being in the Now. He reminds me that true innocence can only exist in this new moment. What a beloved grace. Promptly he has fetched me back home again. I close my eyes and instantaneously fall off the edges of my hard-worn earthly existence into the domain of the heavenly abodes.

CONGRATULATIONS! YOU JUST EXPERIENCED A DOG MOMENT. NOW

The dog angels guard you jealously, keeping the past and the future at bay with the help of magic stars.

The chocolate-colored bunny who lives under the fir tree outside my office just hopped up to the window. She paused to look up at me, twitched her broad, rusty brown nose, erupted in place with what looked to be a bunny hiccup, then did an abrupt turnaround, stopped to nibble some grass and, just as suddenly, scooted off with the speed she might have mustered if all four dogs were in pursuit. For a moment, time was suspended. I was in awe of my own aliveness. It was as though I had just traveled to the moon and back, so enchanted was I. The power of Now is indescribable — inexplicable. Since its evolution, humankind has been burying itself in the past and promising its trove of contentment to the future. We have forgotten how to be alive in the present. We have become the ghosts of someone we once knew and loved who has since died. We spend our time mourning when we could be living. Our dogs are instant reminders, our canine calendars of today. They always come to our rescue and guide us back to our seat — the seat of our souls.

When I realize my days are primarily made up of tasks I no longer enjoy or anticipate with pleasure, but find

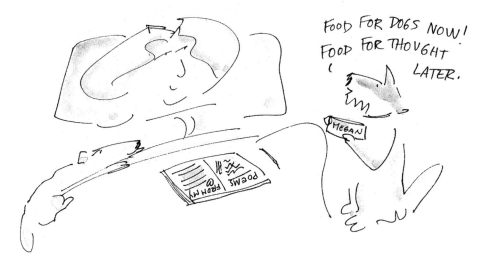

myself muttering, "I just can't wait to get this over with," it is time to reexamine my priorities.

When I find myself thinking that fun and feeling are interfering with my work, it is time to lie down in the lawn with my dogs and ruminate on a blade of grass.

When I'm madly sorting drawings, obsessed and overwhelmed by the drama of the day, Moon approaches with her rubber duck and shames me into submission.

"Mom, priorities please. Time is short and I'm short too, so get down here and throw the duck." How often do we promise to pay attention to the big picture just as soon as we accomplish that one last task?

"Make the list and then bury it," our dogs say. "Stop living life through a straw. Perhaps this pant is the first one and maybe this pant is the last one, so let's go for a walk, see the sky, smell the day, look at the light gauzing through the ferns. Let's take a nap. Let's answer that distant bark with one of our own. Arf! Come taste this. Violets are delicious and I seem to remember you hid a chocolate Santa in the den drawer. Let's curl up together in the sunshine before the sun sets. Let's travel together fearlessly in the Now. Let's woof with the pleasure of becoming whole again."

As I sit at my computer, shoulders slowly creeping earward, Muse presses her cold nose against my thigh. I stop and our eyes engage. She becomes my mirror of the moment. So I lean back in my chair and invite her to climb up on my lap. Here we can share the view of the green vista. Together we admire the reflection of the still naked branches of the fig tree flirting with spring. Their braided limbs appear to be shimmying as two ducks launch them-  selves into the pond and set it a swirl. Muse snuggles in closer, her warm fur tickling a little, then we spot the fat, brown bunny luxuriating expansively on the lawn under her tree. "Lucky you have no interest in chasing her," I tease. "She has gotten too fat to hop very fast." As if in agreement, Muse tucks her head under my chin. "I am the love bulletin," she announces with a shy smile and winks her funny blond eye that gets sunburned in the summer. "Love me. Nothing else matters in this moment. Everything else is a fantasy. Love me now." Her smile is patient but holds the potential of turning into tears. I understand. It reflects the origin of my own sadness, born out of the bitter sweetness and fleeting nature of life. It leads me back to my heart, which leads me back to this moment, which leads me back to my dogs and their all important message — to love and be loved is our priority, not in the days ahead but right here and right now.

Our dogs never expend more energy anticipating something than they do fulfilling the actual performance of the task. They have taught me it is time to wake up when: I find I've eaten a whole meal but don't remember swallowing even once; I'm standing by the Xerox machine with glazed-over eyes and papers

flying, bumping into walls and spilling tea; I've arrived at my destination and feel as though the car drove itself; I am precariously changing gears while clenching my cell phone with my shoulder and cricking my neck. Dogs to the rescue. Moon's sweet and wise countenance pops up and I picture her standing there in gentle reprimand, yellow squeaky duck firmly implanted in her mouth, ready to play. And I know what I must do. I slow down, hang up the phone, turn off the music, open the window, and inhale a deep, delicious breath of tangy spring air. For this moment I am at peace with myself and at one with the whole world. "Please cut in," I gesture to the roadster approaching on my left. "I'm in no hurry. Getting there is not my priority."

If there really is a time and a place for everything, our dogs know the time is now and the place is here. Our canine guardians are truly mirrors of the moment. Their reflection, even in our mind's eye, has the power to reawaken our souls to what matters, what is really important in our lives. This takes me back to one of my mother's favorite sayings in the mindfulness parlance of the 1950s, "When in doubt, stop and look for your hostess."

I guess our moms were almost as wise as our dogs. As my dog Muse likes to put it, "In the Now, illumined by the light of our love for each other, we can fulfill our capacity for passion and joy, creativity and insight. We are all lovely creatures."

She has taught me how to leave back then and over there to those foolish folks who aren't lucky enough to live with any dogs.

"We are all lovely creatures."

CHAPTER 7

LOYALTY

A dog will never break your heart, betray your trust, or abandon you when you are needy and afraid, in the throes of madness, or drowning in the lagoon of your emotions.

Boundaries schmoundaries. Constancy is what counts.

WE ARE ONE.

Dogs are loyal and nonjudgmental. We rely on them without question. While we continue to doubt most aspects of our lives, our love tryst with our dog companions is unarguably secure. Their loyalty and obedience inspire us to renewed faith and belief in the nature of our existence. They demonstrate that, "Yes! There is still goodness to be found in this world. Just don't give up yet."

In the land of the canine conspiracy, giving and being of loyal service is better than receiving and tallying up the receipts of debts owed. And it pays over-the-moon dividends. If there is a drawback, it is simply that dog years go too fast or perhaps that human years go on for too damn long.

Our dogs will never poison love's virtue. Through their eyes, we are perfection incarnate.

As we learn to emulate the loyalty of our four-legged friends, we begin to rediscover the gift of true intimacy and faithfulness that result from hanging in there, no matter what fate dishes out.

When I look in the mirror, some mornings I see beautiful and handsome, others perky and youthful, or inevitably old and tired, depending on the changing factors of my inner and outer environment and the varying influences of current times. When our dogs look at us, they see their beloveds. They love us as we are and regard our maturation with the same respect and appreciation they would a good bone, unearthed and aged to its quintessence.

Who else would guide us blindly (sometimes literally, always figuratively) and selflessly through the travails of an indifferent world? Our dogs become our eyes and ears and are always the masters of our hearts and souls. They lead us through muddy waters with resolute commitment and go down the rabbit hole

I LOOKED DOWN THIS MORNING
AND MY KNEES
HAD AGED.

NONSENSE,
THEY ARE PERFECTION.

for us time and again. Without recrimination, they wait all day for our return, nose pressed against the French door, patience and allegiance engraved on their adorable faces.

RIPE BUT NOT
(OVERDONE)"

Sometimes we feel unworthy of such abject consideration. But our dogs teach us that every human creature is deserving of love and loyalty. Their unaffected and unerring example gives us cause to cultivate these true blue traits as a way to live without feeling over-made-up in our hearts.

When I have to go somewhere sans dog, it is with a pang of regret that I make my departure. I wave good-bye to that sweet dedicated little face at the door and say "thanks" for the reminder to be true in all my interactions today, to relax my own judgment, and cultivate my dog-like tendencies.

Even after a long sojourn, my dogs greet my return with loyal frivolity and gracious acceptance of my absence. I still feel guilty (being under the sentence of my human shortcomings) and offer a bribe of carrots and cookies in exchange for a little more selfish time to nest, listen to messages, change my clothes, return phone calls, and generally engage in the quaint ritual tasks of the worker, which give me

FRUITY BUT SUBTLE,
POSSESSING A CERTAIN
TANGY" JE NE SAIS QUOI...

HOW CAN YOU
MISS HER SO
WHEN SHE HAS
BEEN HARDER
ON YOU THAN
THE PASSAGE
OF TIME?

YOU WOULDN'T
UNDERSTAND.
IT'S A
DOG
THING.

Greeted with loyal frivolity.

huh" while working a crossword puzzle.) Down relates, "Very interesting. Now it's time to take you out for an airing, doncha think?" (By that time your friend has ambled mindlessly off to the bathroom, leaving you hanging midsentence.)

Our dogs trust us. They don't question our intentions. They make us feel good about ourselves, and we are better people because of them. They quell our skepticism. A true dog lover would never pose the question: "Where has that nose been?" Just like our dogs, we choose to shrug blithely. "Who cares, nuzzling up is what is paramount."

Dogs are guileless, free of the bondage of judgment. We are shackled by the cynic within and intimidated by the critic waiting out there to pounce. Such condemning of ourselves, each other, and life's spontaneity robs us of the ability to connect and experience our true unity.

Our dogs' equanimity and loyalty can expunge the poisons from our souls, reawaken our loving spirit, and point the way to the road of happiness. Its stepping stones are loyalty to

CARRY ON. I'M HANGING ON YOUR EVERY WORD.

Where has that nose been?

RHETORICAL, RIGHT?

our true heart song, to our loved ones, and most importantly to our dogs. Our dogs show us how to walk paw in paw with each other through this world of vicissitudes. They are faithful to the end.

CHAPTER 8

DOG AT PLAY, DOG AT REST

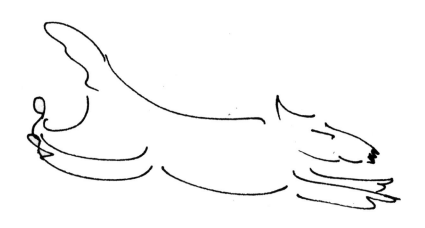

Dogs at play are like angels spinning through rainbows in the sky. Dogs at rest are as tranquil and serene as babies pillowed at their mother's bosom. Dogs don't need martinis to enjoy a happy hour. They prefer a romp in the late afternoon sun where they can dance with their shadows, chase a squirrel, and create chaos on the lawn. Dogs have no need for the pick-me-up of espressos we habitually imbibe to induce a greater state of alertness or for the intoxicants on which we depend to help us relax and calm down after a hard day. Mindfulness and ease of well-being are basic ingredients in canine chemistry. Dogs are naturally high on life, and it is time we learned to look up and follow their example.

Free of drivenness, dogs are able to tire themselves out in the pursuit of their passions and feel better for it. Intense activity segues naturally to a state of complete repose. Unlike human fatigue, which makes us feel tired and wired, our dogs know when to lie down and how to rejuvenate themselves. They have the ability to just let

Dog at rest.

Dogs at play.

SIGH!
RUN? SLEEP? EAT? CUDDLE?
WHAT NOW? . SIGH. IT'S A
DOG'S LIFE!

OK " WHAT'S
TODAY'S STRATEGY?

Dog eating a lemon.

those "zzzzzzz's" flow without sleeping pills, warm milk, chamomile tea, or valerian tinctures. Then with a fulsome stretch and right on schedule, they get up and start all over again refreshed and renewed.

Our furry free-flying friends are natural party animals. They are both instant play stations and walking sanctuaries of repose. They will gladly share our chips, cookies, and ice cream cones when we need that amorphous something — and it has nothing to do with fuel — but their desires are simple, and readily met by whatever is handy. A stick, old bone, piece of rope, your own tail will suffice and provide stimulation and happy amusement.

There we are bumping around groggily in the wee hours and desperately brewing that first cup of coffee or tea so we can surmount the morning inertia and address the day. (Silence will be observed until after the first cup is consumed.) Meanwhile the pack is gnawing at the muzzle and just barely able to control their wildly wagging rears until the den door is opened, and they are free to dash out to explore the enchantment of the morning.

Bow tie.

Adults are tired all the time because our minds are always running. Our dogs know how to say "heel" to their minds. When they run, it feels like the wind cleansing itself and the waves throwing off all

Playing your dog like a lute.

Dog eating your bow tie in lieu of a bone.

inhibition as they embrace the shore. Then without worrying about whether they deserve to take a break, they circle, make a furrow in their chosen nest, and plop down to enjoy a rapturous rest.

Dogs know how to have fun for free and it is catching. We pay a lot to enjoy ourselves, financially, emotionally, and energetically. Instead, at any moment we could look to our pooch and be taken on a gleeful adventure.

"Consume a daily dose of silliness," they instruct us. "Nonsense is full of nutrients and is easy to digest. It gives you energy and enables you to metabolize all of life's other experiences with mirth, contentment, and complete satisfaction. And balance is everything," they add. "Remember, in order to play well, you

Is a cactus less relaxed than a willow?

must learn how to relax like a dog." Their joys and sorrows are translated into healthy games. Play and rest are as distinct and beautifully arranged as the markings on their coats.

Dogs never outgrow their puppy natures or find themselves short of a toy. We are their favorite amusements, but when we won't play they launch themselves into the game of the moment with whatever is at hand. If nothing is going on, well, time to take a nap, curl up, tuck in, and dream. No angsting in front of bad TV or looking for a fun fix. Resting is a noble occupation and playing successfully a victory.

Dogs muse as well as amuse themselves and us, endlessly. At twelve years, Morgan still exhibits puppylike traits. His eyes are as cloudy as sea marbles. His nose can hardly discern where the biscuit fell, when it misses his mouth. But when he trots in and rolls on his back, exposing his soft, tubby, curly belly ("It's all muscle, Mom") and flails his paws about invitingly, he reminds me of the day we brought him home. He emits a soft grr-purr sound, which indicates some stroking is in order, then decides to seize the ball I offer and balances it above his nose,

If you can't be silly, then just don't call me.

his paws juggling the small globe in the air. I laugh out loud. The spirit of playfulness has entered me, and I am immediately enlivened, relaxed, and easy in my being. Our dogs are paragons of innocence and delight, and continue to hold us in awe of the inexhaustible possibilities of this game of life. They remind us that sometimes we just need to do what we want to do instead of what we have to do.

TICKLE ME.
RIGHT HERE MOM.

Moss no longer inhabits her dog body but her memorable manners and unique style live with us like friendly ghosts. She was a puppy and a player to the end, and boy, could she sleep. The house might implode and Moss would dream on blissfully. She was the chunk bunny of the litter and often stubborn and ornery, but too adorable to admonish. She didn't walk, she ambled and carried her head atilt. Deafness and old age didn't limit her natural ability to be a puppy dog of elaborate tricks and infinite invention. Creativity could have been her nom de plume.

INHALING, I AM FULL OF ACCEPTANCE. EXHALING, I AM FREE OF RESISTANCE.

In her youth, Moss fetched relentlessly. Given the opportunity she would retrieve the ball until she dropped, with no ill effects.

Once when we were having our house remodeled and our carpenter friend was in evidence in all rooms, at all hours, seemingly a part of the family landscape, Moss decided to adopt him and assign him the esteemed role of chief ball thrower. As soon as she realized he couldn't always engage in her game and take her trophy because his hands were full of tools, she acquired the habit of pressing the ball between his legs and waiting. A long time. Without blinking.

This became known as Mossbag's Magic Nose Debacle. To his credit, our builder-friend treated this obligation with the proper attitude of noblesse oblige. After all, such a distinction bestowed was nothing short of being put on the honors list, and it boasted the added benefit that no one was required to spoil the fun by acting pompous.

You can imagine the surprise of well-attired guests when they felt the sudden pressure of a round object pressed between their thighs, especially when Moss stealthily approached from the rear. Whether indignant or in appreciation of a cheap thrill, our guests were never bored.

When Moss would join in the fun, even if her arthritic zaftig self wasn't up to ball tricks anymore, she was resourceful and stood with authority, expanding the largesse of her personality to command the stage of life. Moss was one of the few dogs I have known who could take ten curtain calls with an air of ennui and sport a grin so broad and beamy it caused her to sneeze.

Nose in bum, tail in neutral.

When I hear my mind bleat, "What's the point? It's all just too much hard work!" then all I have to do is picture Moon romancing her dinner dish and piling on the fuzzy elephant, rubber duck, and squeaking ball, or Mulph hunkered down with her bone under the redwood tree, or call forth the image of all four dogs romping with me down the road to the creek. We are in nirvana swept aloft by the intoxicating smells, the hot sweet breath of summer air, and the magical sight of the Romney sheep, llama, Angora goat, and Indian antelope racing in circles around the field.

ACHOO!

Dogs know how to take life seriously without taking themselves seriously. They bow down to the gift of life's surprises without putting on the constricting suit of earnestness. They never embarrass themselves and know the healing power of laughter and irony. All their bones are tickle bones.

"Humor brings under-standing," they arf. "That's what I like about being a dog. It softens the truth without compromising it and dashes my arrogance. I always like myself better after a full day of dogging around, and I like you better too. If we can't laugh at our-selves, what's the point? Forget about your gut and always trust your dog."

JE T'ADORE.

JE TE LA FENÊTRE.

Having fun with a pun.

When your human is in the doldrums, put her underpants on your head.

Life is just a ratbag sans cartoons.

People have plenty of practice at being childish, but are very rusty when it comes to being childlike. A dog's playful nature is seductive. They inspire us to cultivate our childlike qualities and to realize we never have to outgrow the wonder of life. We can dance in the surf and dare to get our hems wet and our faces smudged with nature's signature. We can pirouette under the full moon, twirl like the tumbleweeds, sing in the street, smile at a grump, and offer a hug to a stranger.

Our dogs are forever reminding us how to laugh at our own jokes, even when we are aware of missing our tails. They teach us that life never has to feel dull. Playing with our dogs shows us how to unearth the hidden gem of joy that glows in every breath, and shimmers in every single moment. "Play hard and rest heartily," they woof. "Take second helpings. Life is a plaything. Don't put off the chance to live to your capacity. Wrap your laughing gear around every opportunity to come out and play with me. Bring your heart along and your smile. Your dog is invited too."

After all without exception, we are each destined for a long, uninterrupted sleep, so stop the race, and learn to perfect the art of dog at play and the triumph of dog at rest. There is always fun to be had if you'll just take a chance and unleash your inner dog.

Playing well is still the best revenge.

A TAIL TO WAG.

WORLD PEACE.

DOG AND HIS MAN FILLING A STAR WITH WISHES.

A DOG WHOSE FLUIDITY MAKES HIM MORE FUN.

A WOMAN AT HOME IN THE MOON.

SIGH! I WANT TO SOAR, TOO.

MUMPF!

MOSS FILLED WITH ENVY.

AFTERWORD

IN MEMORY

Megan was my spirit dog. From the beginning, she wore her dog suit awkwardly.

We were so symbiotic, I often forgot she was of the canine persuasion and was taken aback when she exhibited doggie behavior like digging a hole or bringing me a ball. It seemed to strike her as odd too, for on these rare occasions, suddenly all tail-wagger activity would cease as though she had caught sight of her reflection in the mirror and realized she was out of character. Then she would promptly drop the ball and with a look of distaste and a "Ptui!" deftly shed the dog image and assume her lying-on-the-chaise-lounge-nibbling-bonbons true persona.

Megan enjoyed food like a gourmand, but ate it like a gourmet. She had the figure and carriage of a great diva. When she wanted to kiss me, I was expected to offer my cheek (which I did gratefully) and received a tongue caress so delicate and thoughtful, she might have been licking a candle flame without making it quiver. Her cuddles were all containing. They felt soft and safe, the way I always imagined it would feel to be held in the protective embrace of the Universal Mother.

CVDDLED

AND

SAFE

Two years before Megan left us, she lost a hind leg to cancer. She continued to carry herself with proud posture and perfected a hop-run that was both efficient and chic. To the end she remained true to her unique style. For Megan, standards never slipped.

Caring for her was an honor. Being selfless in her service expanded my heart. She offered me an enlightened perspective that transformed the spectre of impermanence into the magical experience of being fully alive in the moment, where time ceases to exist.

When the hour came to say good-bye, our eyes locked. Together we looked into infinity. For a moment, we shared our breath and pressed the veil.

Megan died the year before my mother. I am sure she and my mom are out there somewhere in the vastness laughing together, eating ice cream, not exercising, and not cleaning their teeth. I delight in this picture and know absolutely that dogs are angels with fur and a tail, the real guardians of our hearts and souls.

PRESSING THE VEIL

🐾 ACKNOWLEDGMENTS

Loving wags and timeless thanks to Megan, Moss, Morgan, Moon, Muse, and Mulph and to my biggest devoted companion (albeit somewhat less furry) Robert. Grateful wags to Mary Ann Casler. Woofie gratitude to my fearless, remarkable, creative savior and editor Georgia Hughes and everlasting, joyous barks to all canine souls near and far, big or small, born or yet to be born, with tails short or long. May you continue to thrive. Thank you for selflessly guiding us home again and again.

Qui m'aime, aime mon chien.

☙ ABOUT THE AUTHOR

Mari Gayatri Stein has published seven books, and her illustrations have graced the pages of more than thirty books for Nolo Press. Galleries throughout the western United States have exhibited her drawings and her work has appeared in *Tea Magazine, Turning Wheel,* and the East Bay's *Inquiring Mind.* She has also been a teacher of yoga and meditation for many years. Her last book, *The Buddha Smiles: A Collection of Dharmatoons,* was published in 1999 by White Cloud Press. She lives with her husband and four border collies on their fifty acre organic farm and nursery in southern Oregon.

THE MAGNIFICENT BALANCING BUTTERFLIES.

DELICIOUS, COOL POND.

BON BONS

WISHING STARS & BANANA MOONS

SUN OF ILLUMINATION

CLOUDS THAT WILL DISGUISE THEMSELVES AS BUNNIES, BEARS AND BIRDS.

IT'S A DOG'S LIFE. (A TYPICAL DAY.)

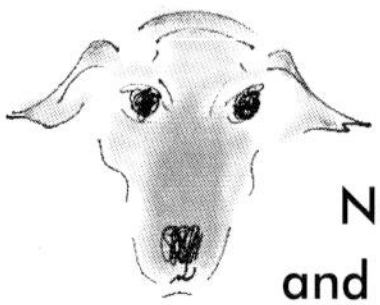

New World Library publishes books
and cassettes that inspire and challenge
us to improve the quality of our lives and the world.

Our books and tapes are available
in bookstores everywhere.
For a free catalog of our complete library
of fine books and tapes, contact:

New World Library
14 Pamaron Way
Novato, CA 94949

Phone: (415) 884-2100
Fax: (415) 884-2199
Or call toll free (800) 972-6657
Catalog request: Ext. 50
Ordering: Ext. 52

E-mail: escort@nwlib.com
Web site: www.newworldlibrary.com

ADIEU.